Oscar Enrique Correa Miranda
Nieves Melo

Computing

Oscar Enrique Correa Miranda
Nieves Melo

Computing

Free Software

ScienciaScripts

Imprint

Cover image: www.ingimage.com

This book is a translation from the original published under ISBN 978-613-9-44175-4.

Publisher:
Sciencia Scripts
is a trademark of
Dodo Books Indian Ocean Ltd. and OmniScriptum S.R.L publishing group

120 High Road, East Finchley, London, N2 9ED, United Kingdom
Str. Armeneasca 28/1, office 1, Chisinau MD-2012, Republic of Moldova, Europe
Printed at: see last page
ISBN: 978-620-8-23359-4

TABLE OF CONTENTS

CHAPTER I

NIEVES MIRANDA

The computer science nowadays represents a hope for the nations of the world, to be able to process data through electronic devices is a fascinating reality, in most universities computer science is studied in the first semesters, in order to be able to give the students strong tools that allow them to perform adequately in their university studies.Computer science can involve studies linked to word processing, calculations, databases and information technology in general. In this research, applications are developed for the internet and smartphones, which allow the study of geometry, the calculation of logarithms and probabilities. The aim is to provide computer science students with technological tools, so that they can better approach the concepts related to mathematics and software development.In this way, through the programmes for the study of geometry developed in this research, students will be able to understand that there is a circle, which has a radius and a diameter; that within a Cartesian plane a movement can be simulated that can lead to collisions or intersections. In this research a computer application is developed, which allows the development of a logarithmic equation based on the search of data information within two variables, something that is fundamental for the understanding of computer science in students of a course. The study of a variable, which in the beginning can be the way to find a piece of information that, when processed and interpreted, becomes relevant information that allows to give an answer to a question posed in the field of their university studies, internships or degree thesis.An application is also developed that allows the study of probabilities, in that sense, three options can be evaluated at any given time, in order to determine the probability of occurrence of an event according to the values assigned to each of these options within the computer system that has been developed.This application for the study of probability can also be considered useful in the case of social networks, to take into consideration for example the probability of increasing the number of users within the social network, the probability that the content offered is of quality, the probability that the interaction with the application of the artificial intelligence system is high, and by taking into consideration the two previous elements, to evaluate the probability that users decide to share the content they have assimilated within the social network.

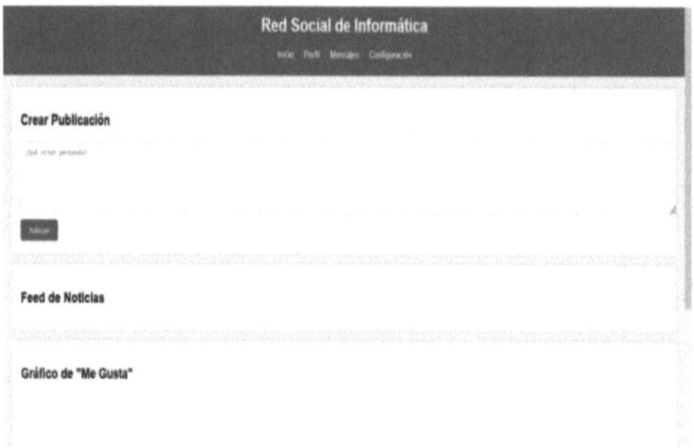

Source: https://intinformatic.blogspot.com/ Social Network.

The aim of this research is to disseminate the importance of the use of internet networks for knowledge management in computer science, which is why a system is developed for the internet that integrates a blog, a social network and mathematical calculators to understand qualitatively and quantitatively everything related to computer science. In this model, applications are developed for the study of geometry, the calculation of probabilities and logarithms, which can be fully applied to a social network, because it is possible to develop educational applications that, when integrated into a social network, allow people to take advantage of their useful time to generate learning around computer science or mathematical concepts that are developed within this model.

Source: https://intinformatic.blogspot.com/ Grafico.

This research deals with probability equations in terms of the occurrence of certain events, taking into consideration two variables and the possible occurrence according to the occurrence of one of the events involved in those variables. Today's information technology with its processing power can definitely help to improve climate development, e.g. certain indicators can be taken into consideration in a given project. The planting of new trees would be an eminently quantitative activity, with the probability of occurrence of a higher level of awareness on the part of people about the environment, which in theory could trigger probabilistically speaking an event that tends to improve the environment. In this research, a calculator is developed in order to establish probabilistic variables and events, which, with the use of computers, will definitely improve the environment.

Source: https://intinformatic.blogspot.com/ App Social Network.

In the development of this investigation it is possible to establish an application that is sustained in a server, in order to be able to spread the mathematical and computer probabilistic knowledge that is intended to strengthen the knowledge of students, teachers and managers in general lines of different institutions.

The advantage of being able to develop this type of applications is that people from their smart phone systems can access these calculation tools and thus be able to try to understand the various processes that occur in their companies, universities or organisations, taking into consideration the powerful level of technology that can be handled with the use of languages. programming, which today are based on neural and quantum processors.

Source: https://intinformatic.blogspot.com/ Generator

The research develops the algorithm, which in theory allows the calculation of the greatest common divisor of two numbers, but in this case it is intended to be applied to a search for values within a search scheme that assesses the possibility of finding a value within a series of successive numbers or variables set within the system.

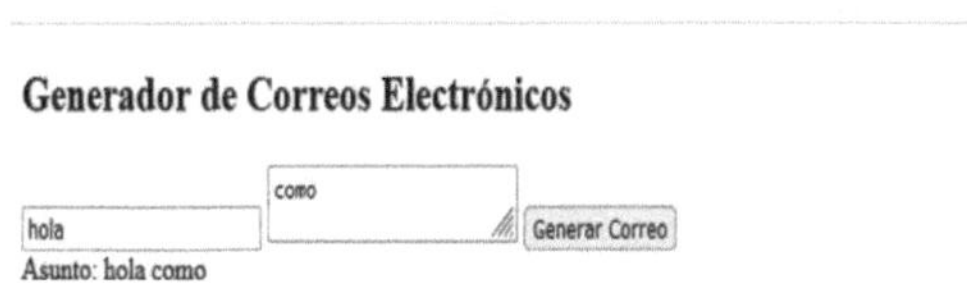

Source: https://intinformatic.blogspot.com/ Generator.

The research develops Bayes' Theorem, which, for example, makes it possible to deal with the probability of contamination with respect to a component of the environment. In the research, programmes are developed that can contribute to the interconnection between people, for example, with the use of an e-mail generator that can work from a server, in order to provide the support to people that is so important at this time. It should be noted that this type of technology at the beginning of the 21st century was a pioneer in communication between people, and today it is still fully relevant to the extent that it has an impact on the way transactions are carried out at a global level in the various financial interconnection systems and platforms.

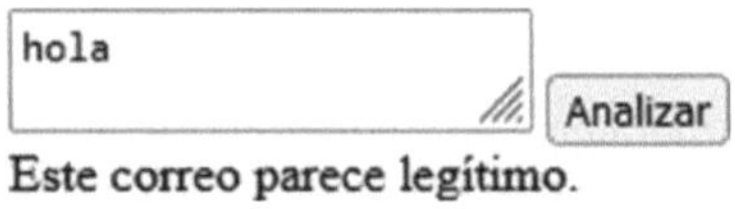

Source: https://intinformatic.blogspot.com/ Detection.

It is extremely important to incorporate Bayes' theorem in the development of an e-mail system, as it will allow the real possibility of detecting unwanted e-mails in the system, in order to guarantee the secure use of the e-mail system in communications between people. Every day more and more people go online to disseminate information that is inappropriate or simply unwanted advertising to people, definitely integrating probabilistic calculations to determine the probability that an email represents unwanted advertising, which will contribute positively to the success and security of the email system that we are trying to implement, understanding that security is nowadays fundamental in an interconnected world where there are different commercial and personal interests.In this case, a system was developed that allows to calculate, based on Bayes' theorem, the probability of occurrence of a given event at some point in time. On the screen it can be seen that the probability that event A occurs is evaluated by assigning it a value of 0.5, the probability that event B occurs by assigning it a value of 1, the probability that B occurs because A has occurred was given a value of 1, from this we proceed to calculate the probability that event A occurs because B has occurred, it is obvious that the result is 0.5. It is really wonderful to be able to have these probabilistic theories, which with the use of this programme will allow us to simulate possible situations that may occur at some point, such as the level of contamination of a river, or the probability of certain special processes occurring within a processor or a computer system.

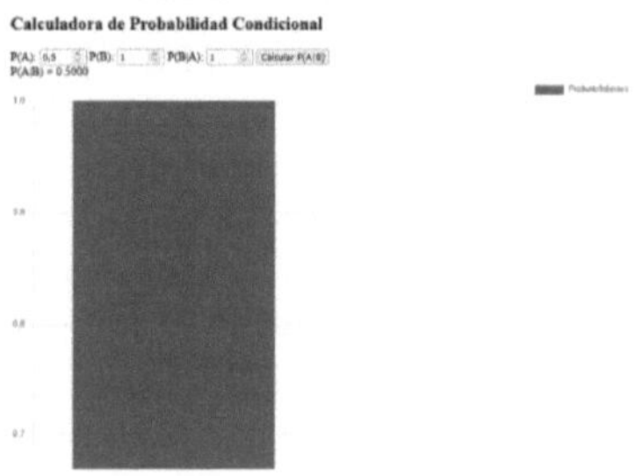

https://intinformatic.blogspot.com/2020/10/prrincipal.html Probability.

When we refer to probabilistic events, we have to take into consideration certain circumstances that may arise. In this sense, experience shows that when teaching a computer science class, for example, there are many students who have high expectations of taking this curricular unit, and it is definitely necessary to incorporate the technological elements of hardware and software in the teaching process so that they can adequately empower themselves with this knowledge that is so fundamental for their lives. It is always necessary when approaching a teaching process in computer science to take into consideration motivation, which, according to experience, can only occur to the extent that the leader of the educational process, or teacher, is able to demonstrate that he or she possesses the necessary motivation to teach. The students will be able to understand that the contents being taught can be of great use for their student and professional life.

It is necessary to point out that, if there is the right level of motivation and it is transmitted in the right way, all computer science students in a university course will be able to feel through group integration that the information they are receiving can be of great use to them.In this sense, it is recommended to encourage group integration, they can have the ability to set up work teams in order to be able to visualise the multimedia contents that are being taught in the IT curricular unit, use the technological means to assimilate and put this knowledge into practice; so that at the end of each curricular unit they can present a practical evaluation that allows them to assimilate the content that is being taught in the context of their student or professional life.

When students realise that there is a so-called group integration, that the contents are easily accessible and can be developed by themselves through their work teams, that they have a goal based on a specific time frame in which they have to hand in the assignment, and that they will be assessed on the basis of the results they have generated. Surely there will be a fairly participative dynamic in which the level of probability that the requirements will be met on time, that the content they present will be of quality, and that therefore the results expected quantitatively at the level of evaluation will be optimal and coherent with the effort they have made.

CHAPTER II

OSCAR ENRIQUE CORREA MIRANDA

When referring to computer science it is necessary to mention a world of dreams, when a computer science teacher is teaching a class he/she can think of smart phone systems, Tablets, Laptops, computers and an endless number of technological elements that nowadays integrated with the internet make it possible for dreams to come true. When a person is in charge of teaching a computer science class, or is generating a computer science process, it is necessary that they connect with all their personal dreams and that they can transmit them to those who are listening to them. When teaching a computer class it is necessary that the students understand that the time has come to start dreaming, with that independence that they want for their lives, because I came to make a knowledge that can represent the possibility to transform the yearnings into a tangible reality. One of the great dreams that can be planted in computer science students is the possibility of overcoming the traditional distance and time barriers, so that they are able to develop technological programmes, for example, from their computers or smartphones to satisfy the information or product needs of many people in the world. In this sense, dreaming in 2024 of the possibility that students at the end of a computer science course will be able to have tools for mathematical, logarithmic and probabilistic calculation and the study of geometry represents a wonderful training opportunity that, when put into practice through the development of applications, represents the possibility that these students who are receiving theoretical knowledge can go from being management advisors to becoming active consultants and programme developers who can provide real solutions to a world that is waiting for immediate answers.

https://intinformatic.blogspot.com/2020/10/prrincipal.html Spheres.

Thanks to current programmes and programming languages, mathematical models can be simulated that allow, as in this case, the generation of two spheres, which at some point may collide and update what would be their speed. This type of model can be applied above all to video games, which can be educational in order to train new generations in a positive way in the area of computer science. In this specific case, the programme that has been developed allows students to recognise that there are geometric figures, in this case two circles, and that they can have a speed of displacement that can vary at some point, especially if there is a collision, which would immediately generate the reduction of speed to zero. This type of software allows in an educational way to simulate events that may occur at some point with the displacement of objects within a geographical area, such as cars, motorbikes or bicycles.

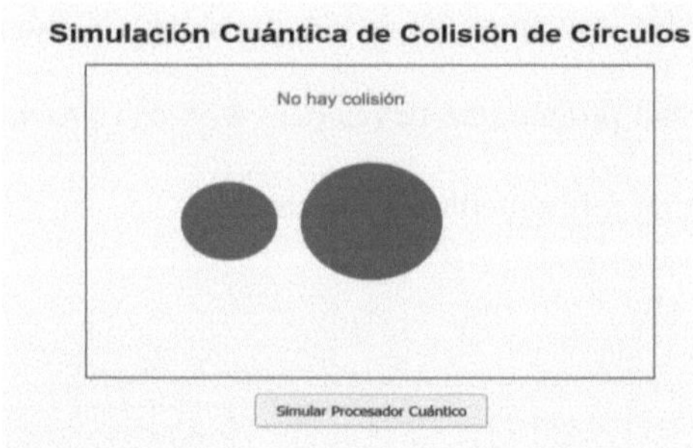

https://intinformatic.blogspot.com/2020/10/prrincipal.html Collision circles.

In the case of quantum processors that represent the possibility of generating computer processes taking into account high processing speeds, a mathematical model was generated that integrates the collision of two geometric figures plus the theory of the probability of such a collision occurring. By applying the mathematical and probabilistic model, the collision of the hypothetical atomic elements that are integrated within the quantum processor is generated as a result in some cases, in order to try to simulate from the computer vision what these quantum processes could be like within a processor of this high level of quality.

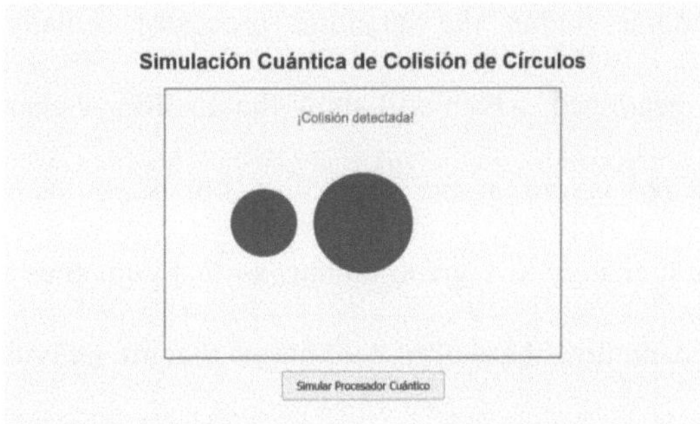

https://intinformatic.blogspot.com/2020/10/prrincipal.html Quantum simulation.

In this case, the quantum collision simulation software inside a quantum processor was able to detect a collision, so the colour of the circles changes from red to green. of qualitative changes in colour and quantitative changes in speed. This type of software model tries to promote motivation in computer science students, so that they can understand that there are programs and operating systems, which allow them with the use of mathematics at some point to try to simulate a situation that is quite abstract, such as the movement of atoms inside a quantum processor. For the generation of this programme, we proceeded to use the high-level programming language based on JavaScript, the start quantum process button was added to start the movement of the spheres within the area that in theory would be the spaces of the quantum processor. We proceeded to simulate the quantum superposition, generating the random movement within the scenario on the screen, which in theory would be the different movements made by the atoms within the quantum processor. Finally, the quantum entanglement is generated, which will show the qualitative change of colour of each atom in a red colour at the beginning, but when the entanglement is produced, it could change to a green colour, so that computer science students can try to understand how these ultra-cold atoms that are individually controlled can generate processes that lead to a higher speed in a computer.

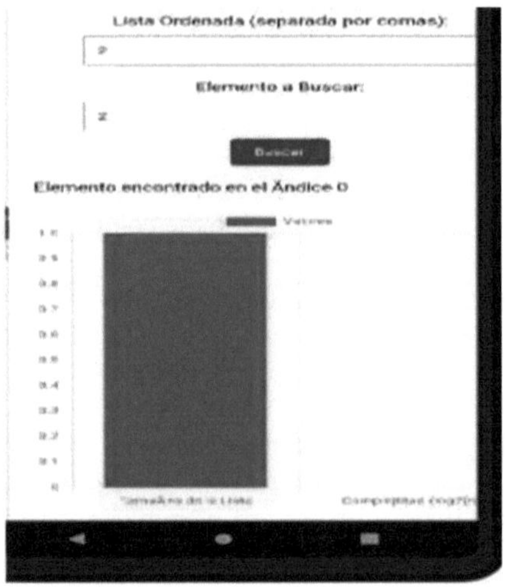

https://intinformatic.blogspot.com/2020/10/prrincipal.html App Item found.

It is important to understand that within computer processes the search for information is a fundamental aspect, in this example reference is made to a Euclidean algorithm, extended that can find the maximum common divisor, and the coefficients of two variables, in order to be able to generate at the end a graphic result of the process carried out. In this case, we proceeded to introduce in The initial value of 2 was entered for the binary search, and the value of 2 was entered as the element to be searched for, thus generating a blue graph, which graphically shows that the element was found in its entirety. This algorithm is definitely wonderful and executed from a computer programme in the form of a phone application, it will definitely teach students that important notion that there can be a piece of data at some point in time within a variable or a database, and that this value can be found specifically through a search procedure which in turn can give a graphical result of the level of compliance of the process and whether it has been executed 100% effectively.

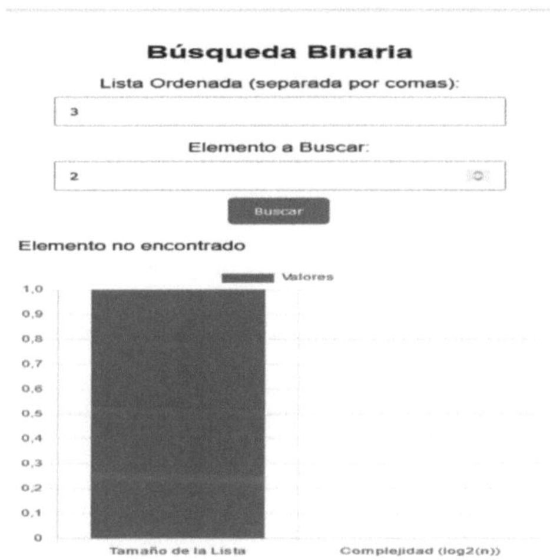

https://intinformatic.blogspot.com/2020/10/prrincipal.html Search.

The development of programmes that allow computer science students to understand the search processes through the extended Euclid's algorithm is fundamental, this type of search is currently highly recognised and the logic of the procedure is immersed from applications that carry out conversations to those programmes in which there are databases that control the inventory of products in a warehouse. In this case we proceeded by introducing different values, which resulted in the programme expressing element not found. When teaching a computer course, there are definitely elements such as file extensions that are tangible concepts, which when taken into consideration allow the student to understand that there are programmes and that each of these programmes generates files, with extensions that can allow different activities to be carried out, such as editing texts, executing calculations or making presentations.Classroom experience indicates that teaching those file extensions linked to each of the computer programmes is fundamental, so that students can understand that the information they perform in those programmes is going to be stored inside a technological device, which can be recognised visually by the file extension and which generates an icon with a certain image that represents it.

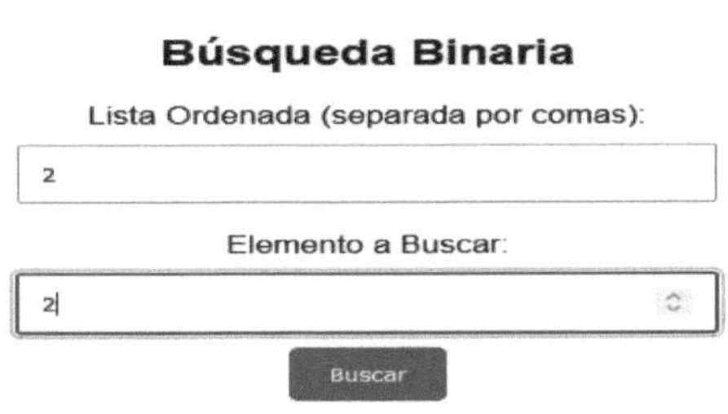

https://intinformatic.blogspot.com/2020/10/prrincipal.html Lista.

When teaching a computer class, it is definitely essential to teach participants that they can search the content they have saved on their computer, as this will allow them to differentiate between a folder and a file, so that they can have a folder identified with a name that represents the type of content they are creating on their computer or smartphone. It is necessary in that sense to teach them to identify that there are videos, images, programme files; that they can be found quickly with the implementation of a search programme either within the operating system or a programme that has been designed to find information, within the computer or smart phone system that is being used.

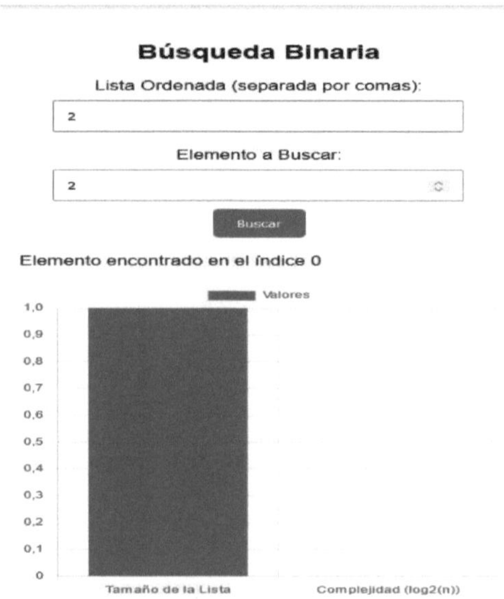

https://intinformatic.blogspot.com/2020/10/prrincipal.html Search.

All these search programmes are extremely important especially for those people who are just starting out in the world of computing, as they may often be able to create an image or multimedia content, which they have managed to save on the computer but are often not fully aware of the exact location or folder where it has been saved. At that point, if the person understands that he/she can search by file extension even if he/she does not remember the file name, he/she will be able to obtain as a result a series of files that have to do with the type of programme he/she wants to find. For example, if a student managed to create a text file on the computer, but cannot find it, with the implementation of this type of search programme, he/she will be able to find it by simply typing the file extension and pressing the search button to obtain the desired result. This research integrates a practical model that through applications allows the calculation of logarithms, probabilities and the study of geometry. In this sense, when the study of the logarithm is approached, it is possible through these equations using the computer tool that was developed in this research or software applied to the search for information within variables. This is something really cool, for example, to be able to evaluate the number of people who have a specific age can be something really relevant in the context of a requirement that an institution or a company demands. There are institutions for example that for certain jobs require people to have a certain age, and through these searches you can try to relate a number with the age of a person to obtain data that can be handled later as useful information for the organisation, especially if you are making reference to what is linked to the recruitment of staff at some point.

https://intinformatic.blogspot.com/2020/10/prrincipal.html Antivirus.

Definitely when referring to computing it is necessary to mention antivirus, which have been evolving to try to give functionality to computers, Tablet,

Laptop and Smartphone systems. Since the 20th century when floppy disk drives were in use, it could be seen how information could be transmitted from 1.44 Mb storage drives, which consisted of floppy disk drives that allowed people to transfer files to hard drives, but also to install programs from those drives. This obviously had the direct benefit that because they were portable they could be moved from one computer to another in an attempt to facilitate operations. This also brought with it the possibility that in some of these information transfers a virus could be present, hidden inside a system file, at that moment it was recommended to have the anti-write tab of the diskette open so that no type of virus could enter, which are the so-called computer programmes that can cause damage to the systems or even to the computer's hard infrastructure units.

Faced with this situation, it was sometimes necessary to activate the floppy disk's tab, so that it could record its information, which meant that at that time it could not only receive certain files but also some kind of virus that could be harmful to the handling of the information.Faced with this situation, developers of antivirus programmes began to emerge, which simply had a database of existing viruses and their possible elimination. In that sense, most of the programmes offered the possibility of a quick or deep scan, everything would depend on the user's time availability, after all, when using this type of antivirus systems, what was required was the activation of the scanning of the storage units, followed by the detection of any existing viruses and the subsequent quarantine of any anomalies found in the system. Nowadays when making direct reference to antivirus it is necessary to mention that there are threats such as: malware, ramsonware that can affect the operation of operating and computer systems. Faced with this situation there are companies and individuals who have decided to protect their systems, it is necessary to highlight that some current operating systems integrate an antivirus system to protect the integrity of hardware devices and software connected to the general system. It is necessary to understand that the internet has come to play a fundamental role in this situation. It is worth noting that many of these antivirus systems currently have the capacity to be updated online, which gives them a very interesting dynamic in terms of their main activity, which is to protect the use of computer systems in real time.

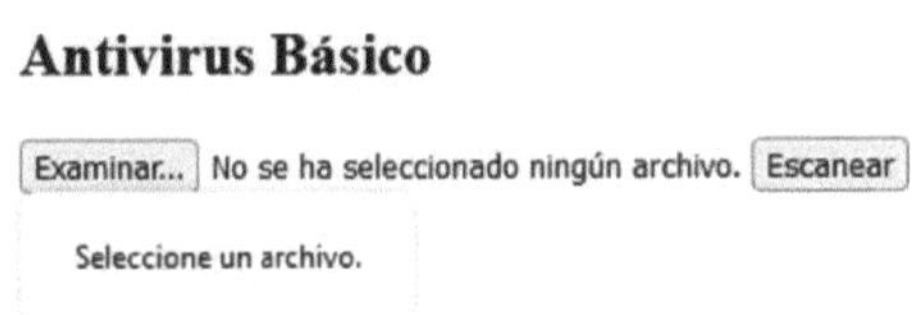

https://intinformatic.blogspot.com/2020/10/prrincipal.html Antivirus.

A good antivirus has to have the real and true ability to scan storage options that might at some point be infected, in that sense internal or external hard drives, removable external storage drives are nowadays subject to scanning and virus detection, in order to maintain the integrity of the operating and functional systems of the computer or smartphone. In that sense, some people nowadays prefer to have real-time detection of viruses or threats on the system in order to prevent physical damage or loss of information.

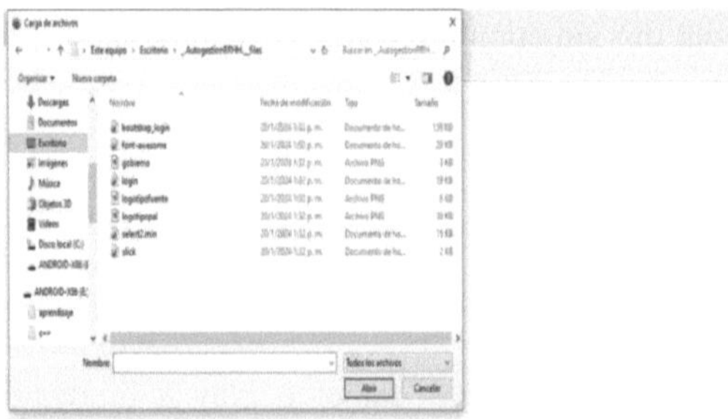

https://intinformatic.blogspot.com/2020/10/prrincipal.html File upload.

Definitely when teaching a computer class it is necessary to show students the different antivirus options available on the market, understanding that there are options that can be free or paid for everything. depending on the needs of the institution or company where the IT activities are being developed. It is necessary to understand that there are anti-virus systems that can often detect programming code as harmful, and pre-emptively proceed to generate a warning.In practice nowadays when developing software based on programming languages such as Java, C++ and others, it is advisable to have the programming codes on a removable external drive to the computer, so that when the antivirus system detects the programming code and considers it to be an abnormal activity, the external storage drive can be removed so that the normal operations of the computer can continue.

https://intinformatic.blogspot.com/2020/10/prrincipal.html Applications.

There are now definitely operating systems that are privately owned and licensed for free distribution, it is necessary to emphasise that in this sense, all of them are The development of applications for smart telephony has been gaining significant space, because this type of technology, which can normally have wireless or satellite interconnection, allows people to make significant progress in all communication, student or work processes, due to its practical form, its significantly smaller size and the possibility of taking it to different places.

At the programming level this represents a truly fascinating challenge, so nowadays with applications such as Java or C++ you can try to create virtual environments that can emulate an operating system such as Android, as the development of applications focused on intelligent mobile phone systems is becoming more and more necessary due to market demand. This is why generating such virtual environments through programming code is truly fascinating, in such a way that once a given application is programmed, whether for educational, organisational or industrial purposes, it can emulate the conditions inside the computer where it is being programmed, even if the operating system is proprietary software.

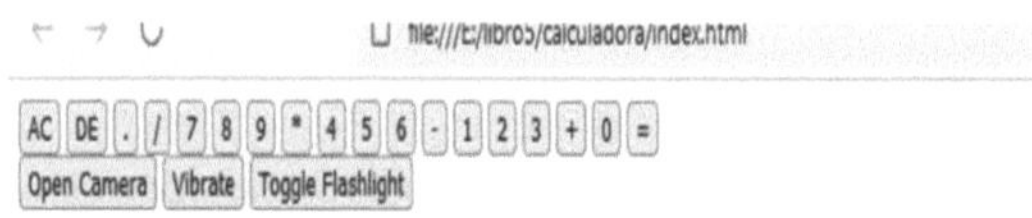

https://intinformatic.blogspot.com/2020/10/prrincipal.html Calculator.

One of the applications that is essential to develop from the point of view of programming code is the calculator, since most operating systems for both computers and smartphones are capable of integrating such a program. In this research we developed a program focused on a calculator, which allows the user to develop different calculations from a web browser. It is a wonderful thing to be able to develop a calculator that can be accessed from a web browser or website, as many computer science students can begin to feel that working on a computer is something that will contribute positively to their student and professional development.

https://intinformatic.blogspot.com/2020/10/prrincipal.html Inference.

Another relevant aspect of computer science education is to be able to teach students that there is a logic to working with either hardware or software components. In this research, a programme was developed that allows people to try to understand how a server works, understanding that nowadays, with technologies such as Apache, the research activity being carried out in a university or institution can be made known to the world.

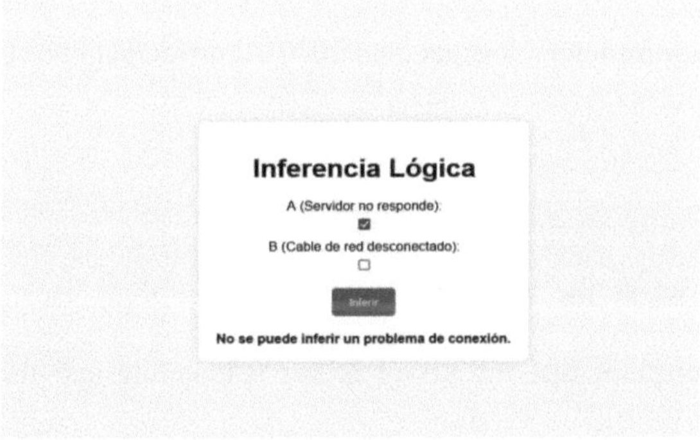

https://intinformatic.blogspot.com/2020/10/prrincipal.html Server does not respond.

In this case, using the logic and the programme developed in this research, when the server does not respond, it is not possible to infer a connection problem. It is necessary to understand that there are times in which a web technology is developed within an Apache server, and depending on certain elements of operability such as memory and storage capacity, it is possible to say that at some point the server will not be able to respond. responds to an instruction given to it through programming code.

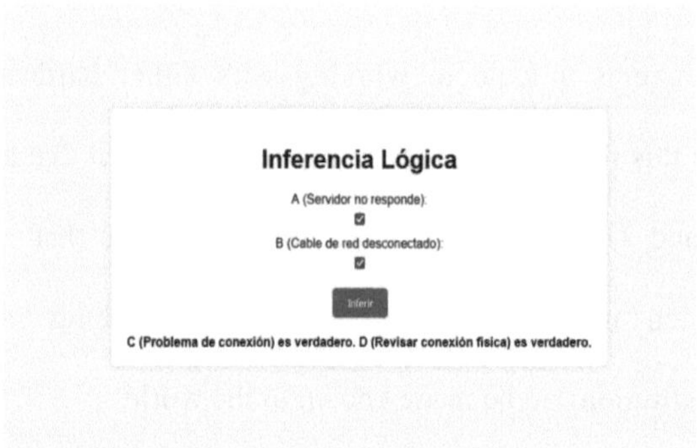

https://intinformatic.blogspot.com/2020/10/prrincipal.html Inference.

In this case, when the programme developed in this research, by logical inference, determines that the server is not responding and that the network cable is disconnected, it proceeds to give a message that the problem is real and checks the physical connection.This type of programme allows computer science students to understand that there is a server, which represents the possibility, through a programme such as Apache, to use the storage space of a computer and to generate web-style behaviour by simulating internet conditions within established structures. Now, conditions such as the response of the server to certain requests made by clients through the internet or intranet are evaluated, but also the physical conditions of the server are evaluated if it has an active and functional connection. In this way, the student can understand each of the parts of the server, but also become familiar with the possibility of a failure and the possible alternatives in such situations.

https://intinformatic.blogspot.com/2020/10/prrincipal.html User.

A key aspect that computer science students need to learn is that today's servers are focused on handling large storage capacities, known as the cloud, so a programmer can develop a software application that is then distributed through global application distribution systems on the internet, thus generating interaction with large numbers of people. Now, most applications focused on e-learning, virtual communication and others take into consideration the possibility of evaluating the user's credentials. This consists in having the ability to evaluate whether a person who is trying to log in to the system is previously registered in a database or variable.

https://intinformatic.blogspot.com/2020/10/prrincipal.html Validation.

In this case, an access system has been developed, which can detect whether a user is allowed to log in or simply cannot log in. Something similar can be observed in today's operating systems, in which refers to the login for a particular user who may have a name, and who must be identified in order to gain access to certain important operating system resources such as the administrator level. Every IT student should understand that there are different levels of access to a particular system, depending on the utility or functionality that each user has to generate within the system. There are cases linked for example to the level of study control in universities, in which teachers can have access to a level that allows them to upload grades into the system and in turn be able to send them to central study control, which must be responsible for processing all those uploaded grades in order to give an effective and valid prosecution to all students within the university.

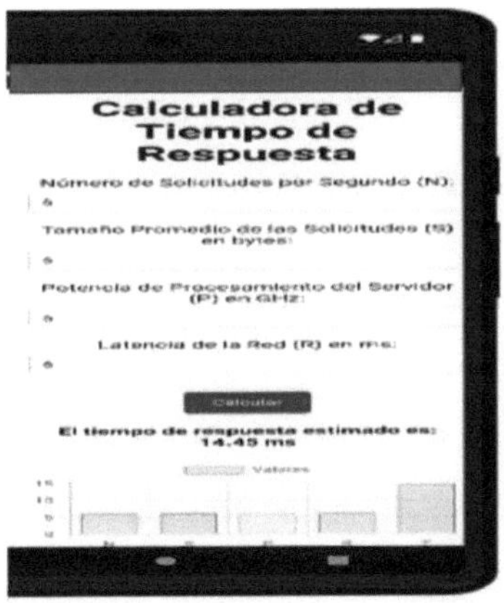

https://intinformatic.blogspot.com/2020/10/prrincipal.html App Latency.

In this research, an application was developed that takes into consideration the number of requests per second, average request size in bytes, server processing power, network latency as a function of response time, which in this case was 14.45 ms.The requests to this server have to do with the way in which a client that is connected through some internet protocol, manages to develop the request for some type of information, in that sense many times a person may require some type of information from the database or calculation that is being executed within the server.

https://intinformatic.blogspot.com/2020/10/prrincipal.html Server processing.

In this type of programme the average size in bytes of the requests that are made is also taken into consideration, in that sense nowadays it can be observed that when developing a programme for example of voice dictation that runs from the server that has been created, that can generate a series of data that is transmitted as a response, it is necessary to understand that many people prefer to use the services of remote servers in some The main reason for this is the transfer speed or the capacity to process data that it possesses. In this research a theoretical model is developed that involves the study of geometry, the calculation of the logarithm and probabilities. In this sense, for example, the response probabilities of a server can be evaluated, taking into account the network connection, the programmes they have and the number of requests made by the clients. In this sense, other important elements could be included, such as the introduction of artificial intelligence programmes that run from servers, many of which in most cases require advanced neural or quantum processors or the integration of GPU cards to be able to generate a better response. In the sense of probabilities, to the extent that technologies are incorporated that process a greater amount of information, with a greater number of speed, it is necessary in this case to understand that the speed of response to the client may be of better quality.

https://intinformatic.blogspot.com/2020/10/prrincipal.html Average applications.

It is necessary to understand that when you have created a server based on Apache technology, you can establish a main page in HTML format, which will be the formal presentation to third parties of all the services that are being offered from the server, in this research for example social networks are developed, online programs for text editing, voice dictation and other applications in terms of computer science. It is necessary to take into consideration that the response to all these processes will depend on the processing speed of the server. The object of study works with a 3 GHz processor model i5, on which the different activities are developed in the different programming languages that have been established through computer codes that are stored on the server as files.

https://intinformatic.blogspot.com/2020/10/prrincipal.html Requests per second.

In terms of network latency, this has to do with the periods of time over which a piece of information that has an internet connection travels, in this case it is measured in milliseconds. In this sense, experience indicates that it is advisable that both connections are supported by a high level of interconnectivity, which in most cases, especially for artificial intelligence applications, is recommended to be higher than 100 MB per second.This research develops a practical model that involves the study of probability, geometry and the calculation of logarithm; in this sense it tries to establish a way for computer science students to understand that through the calculation of the logarithm, information searches can be carried out that analyse two variables at some point in time. This is something truly transcendental in the world of computer science, since data is constantly being transformed into information, so that we can always try to obtain results that are reliable and useful for organisations.

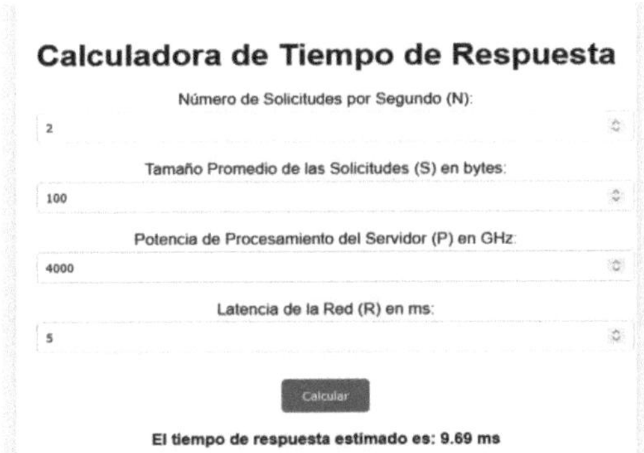

https://intinformatic.blogspot.com/2020/10/prrincipal.html Response time.

It is necessary that all computer science students can understand that most of the processes nowadays are being developed from the internet, there are cases in which the students need to check their grade to the system supported by study control, for this they can access to what is called a main page of the server to be able to enter their password and their key.Once students have logged in, if they have access to a central study control system, they will be able to check their grades, which in most cases are assigned to each curricular unit with five evaluations, which can be considered from 0 to 100, from 0 to 20 or according to the scale that each university has decided to assign.

https://intinformatic.blogspot.com/2020/10/prrincipal.html Response time.

In this case, the programme that has been developed from the server allows people to evaluate a series of variables, which will represent the values obtained as a result of the calculations linked to the server's response speed. This is why the use of neural or quantum processors in the future of computing applied to these artificial intelligence programmes provides a very pertinent response to the need for an efficient response required for the management of information from the client-server level.

https://intinformatic.blogspot.com/2020/10/prrincipal.html Collisions.

In this case, a computer programme was developed so that computer science students can graphically visualise the elements linked to two circles, for which they are asked for the values of the centre of the circle and the radius of the circle, so that they can evaluate the possibility of two circles moving in a given area and at some point in this displacement they can generate a collision.

In this research case, a model focused on the study of geometry, probability and the calculation of the logarithm was developed. It is necessary to understand that probabilistic calculations allow to evaluate the probability of occurrence of an event at a given time. For example, the probability of occurrence of three events can be evaluated, which can often be assigned from a logical perspective or an exhaustive quantitative analysis.

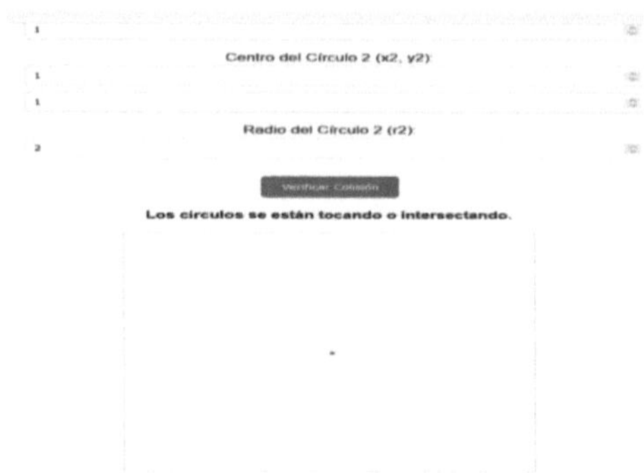

https://intinformatic.blogspot.com/2020/10/prrincipal.html Circles.

In this case it is possible to evaluate whether the circles are touching or intersecting, where intersection is understood as the point at which two circles can touch. In this research a practical model is developed that involves the study of geometry, probability and logarithm calculus. In this sense, we aims to give computer science students the basic notions of a geometric figure as important as the circle, so that they can understand that this figure can have a displacement in a Cartesian plane that in turn has a velocity, which can generate consequences such as collisions or intersections.

https://intinformatic.blogspot.com/2020/10/prrincipal.html Circles.

In this case, a value of 6 was assigned to the centre and radius of the circles, generating the result that the circles are touching each other. It is important that computer science students understand that through the programming language, you can simulate events of reality as in this case the intersection of two circles, obviously this should stimulate the understanding of the importance of using a server that can host files that have programming code in function of simulate situations of reality, and how these computer programmes can be used to respond to everyday situations.

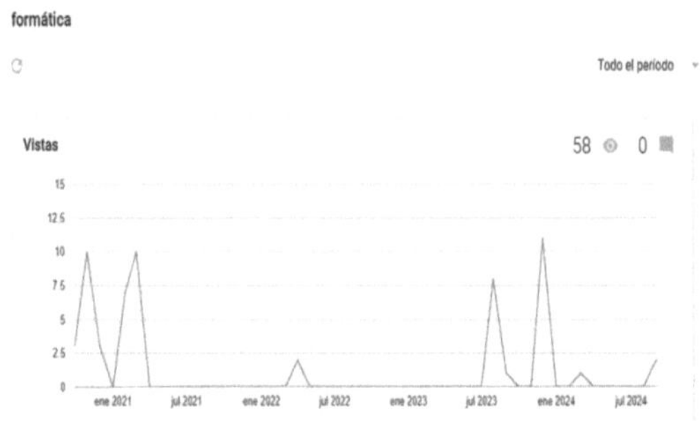

https://intinformatic.blogspot.com/2020/10/prrincipal.html Views

The aim of this research is to promote a model that takes into consideration geometry, logarithm calculation and probabilities, in order to understand all the aspects that can be evaluated in the world of computing, both from a geometric point of view, as well as from searches within variables and probabilistic calculations, in order to understand the reality that is lived day by day and the different circumstances that occur in the world of computing from the point of view of mathematics.Establishing a model of this type will allow students to understand different elements of computer science, so that they can initially can assimilate the different contents that exist in mathematics and statistics, but assimilated from the level of computer programmes and equations that allow the generation of certain simulated processes within virtual environments.

https://intinformatic.blogspot.com/2020/10/prrincipal.html Browsers.

Developing a mathematical model that allows the study of geometry, the probability of occurrence of an event and logarithmic calculations will allow people to understand certain processes that occur today within the internet, in that sense today geometric figures are used as a way to try to ensure that certain processes occur properly within social networks, specifically in the case of the geometric figure when referring to the circles often used the overlapping circles to verify that it is a human being who is using a given system. It is necessary to understand in this sense that such a model applied to computer systems, for example, can be useful in the case of evaluating different probabilistic events that may occur, taking into consideration for example the number of attempts to access a system, if the allowed limit is exceeded, the possibility of generating a message restricting access to the system may occur.

https://intinformatic.blogspot.com/2020/10/prrincipal.html Continents.

In this case, a mathematical model was developed, which integrates computer programmes, in order to solve probability calculations, logarithm equations and the study of geometry. In this sense, the aim is to promote the study of computer science, but also to provide people with technological tools so that they can understand how different processes are generated within computer systems and social networks in general.Being able to develop technological systems that integrate the application of mathematics, represents the possibility for computer science students to begin to study the ways of organising and presenting information, in order to give coherence to all those ideas that can be generated in the field of information. It is necessary to indicate that nowadays educational processes marked by constant innovations are being generated every day, an example of this is the use of artificial intelligence to train students, who are characterised by being informed of the reality through social networks and the internet.That is why every leader of educational processes has to generate interactive processes applied to reality, so that students can get to feel that necessary identification, to have the motivation focused on the curricular units. In this frame of reference, there are already virtual androids with the capacity to generate interaction with students, but that motivational spark today is definitely marked by the example of life and personal commitment that a university teacher can give to his or her class in terms of the educational and professional well-being of his or her students.

https://intinformatic.blogspot.com/2020/10/prrincipal.html Countries.

It is now a wonderful thing for computer science education to be able to develop a model that includes the study of geometry, probabilities and logarithm calculus. In the first instance, to be able to teach computer science students the elements of geometry, and that their behaviour can be studied in a Cartesian plane. As for the study of logarithms, they definitely allow the possibility of comparing two variables, at some point in time, in order to find values that are related. This is a truly wonderful process that is linked to the search for information, which at present can be seen focused from the most basic as the search for a value within a program, trying to find a file within a server or hard drive and of course the most relevant case today which is much broader and has to do precisely with internet searches.

BIBLIOGRAPHICAL REFERENCES

United Nations (2023). Report on Digital Development and Technology Inclusion. Retrieved from https://www.un.org/es/informaticaydesarrollo

United Nations (2022). Strategies for global cybersecurity. New York: United Nations. Retrieved from https://www.un.org/es/ciberseguridad

United Nations (2021). The impact of artificial intelligence on human rights. Geneva: Office of the High Commissioner for Human Rights. Retrieved from https://www.un.org/es/ia-derechoshumanos

United Nations (2020). Technology and sustainable development: A holistic approach. New York: United Nations. Retrieved from https://www.un.org/es/tecnologia-sostenible

United Nations (2019). The digital divide and its impact on economic development. Report of the United Nations Development Programme. Retrieved from https://www.un.org/es/brecha-digital

MIX
Papier aus verantwortungsvollen Quellen
Paper from responsible sources
FSC® C105338

Printed by Books on Demand GmbH, Norderstedt / Germany